DEBUSSY

Oxford Studies of Composers

General Editor: Colin Mason

Egon Wellesz: FUX
Denis Arnold: MARENZIO
Basil Deane: CHERUBINI
Paul Doe: TALLIS
Anthony Payne: SCHOENBERG
Ian Kemp: HINDEMITH
Gilbert Reaney: MACHAUT
Jerome Roche: PALESTRINA
Norman Kay: SHOSTAKOVICH

Oxford Studies of Composers (10)

DEBUSSY

518

ROGER NICHOLS

London

OXFORD UNIVERSITY PRESS

1973

Oxford University Press, Ely House, London W.1

GLASGOW NEW YORK TORONTO MELBOURNE WELLINGTON
CAPE TOWN SALISBURY IBADAN NAIROBI DAR ES SALAAM LUSAKA ADDIS ABABA
BOMBAY CALCUTTA MADRAS KARACHI LAHORE DACCA
KUALA LUMPUR SINGAPORE HONG KONG TOKYO

ISBN 0 19 315426 9

PRINTED IN GREAT BRITAIN
BY EBENEZER BAYLIS & SON LIMITED
THE TRINITY PRESS, WORCESTER, AND LONDON

PREFACE

This short study is necessarily confined to a discussion of Debussy's music at a technical level. The background, the influences, and Debussy's place in the musical world of his time are dealt with only in passing, where they help to illuminate the analytical process. This is not to say that such aspects are irrelevant—they are of course invaluable for a total view of Debussy the artist—but they have already been fully and fascinatingly covered in the work of Edward Lockspeiser. The aim of the present study is to show that 'what fools call Impressionism' has, in Debussy's music at least, a firm technical foundation.

St. Michael's College, Tenbury.   July 1971

CHRONOLOGICAL LIST OF WORKS
DISCUSSED IN THE TEXT

I

In the 1880s the younger French composers were faced with a problem of style. They had of set purpose turned away from the frivolities of Offenbach to the writing of 'serious' music, and Saint-Saëns' foundation of the Société Nationale de Musique in 1871 marks this change of heart with some precision. But on the heels of this renaissance came the sounds of Siegfried's horn, and the age of French Wagnerophilia had begun. So in what style was this seriousness to manifest itself? Saint-Saëns himself clearly chose to remain patriotic, but it is interesting to find that in 1879, before the Wagner craze was really in full swing in France, he was looking to more exotic sources for the new music: 'Tonality, which is the basis of modern harmony, is in a state of crisis. The major and minor scales no longer have exclusive rights. . . . The ancient modes are making a comeback, to be hotly pursued by the scales of the East in all their tremendous variety. All this will strengthen melody in her present exhausted state. . . . Harmony too is bound to change and we shall see developments in rhythm, which has so far hardly been exploited. From all this will spring a new art.' But many others of his countrymen, for longer or shorter periods, succumbed to the charms of leit-motifs and large orchestras, and the merits of Wagner's music were nowhere argued more fiercely than in Paris.

Of course, the younger a composer was the harder it was for him to resolve this dilemma, and for a student at the Conservatoire the problem was particularly acute. While, outside the walls of that and other institutions, the robust qualities of the Teutonic music-drama were beginning to

prevail, inside, Gounod and Massenet taught and perpetu-
ated the classical French virtues of lightness, precision, wit,
and lyrical charm. Nadia Boulanger has related how Gabriel
Pierné, a fellow student of Debussy's at the Conservatoire,
heard the 13-year-old composer improvising on the piano.
His written compositions at that time were poor imitations of
Massenet, but the noises coming from the piano were authen-
tic Debussy. 'Why don't you write like that?' asked Pierné.
'Ah,' said Debussy, 'that is just to amuse the fingers.' For a
composer troubled by his own dichotomies, the general state
of French music at that time was hardly an ideal background,
and it is illuminating to trace Debussy's personal vision
expressed for some time in other men's languages, before it
achieved a speech of its own.

Any assessment of his earliest music is bedevilled by
difficulties of chronology; he revised a lot of his music around
1890. But at least we can say that he was no child prodigy.
His efforts in the early 'teens were anyway directed more
towards a career as a pianist, although by the time he was 16
this goal was already receding from him.

In 1884, at the age of 21, he gained the Prix de Rome with
his cantata *L'Enfant prodigue*, and there can be little doubt
that with this work he was playing by the rules of the establishment (Ex. 1). This extract shows the four-square phrasing,

Ex.1

LIA

A - za-ël,   A - za-ël   pour-quoi m'as tu quit - té - e?

En mon coeur ma-ter-nel ton i - mage est res-tée.

the pleasing melodic line, the merely token counterpoint between voice and violas in bars 5–6, and the anticipatory harmony of the cadence. The unadorned perfect cadence was as abhorrent to him as his impending imprisonment in the Villa Medici and fortunately this harmonic taste was one likely to be shared by his examiners—Gounod among them.

From 1887–9, when he should have been feeding on the cultural atmosphere of Rome and devoting himself to the composition of his statutory *envois*, he embarked with rather more enthusiasm on two sets of songs to poems by Baudelaire and Verlaine, and here for the first time in his music the influence of Wagner becomes apparent, that of *Tristan* in particular. (Ex. 2). This passage from one of the Baudelaire

Ex.2

songs, 'Receuillement', is one of the more obvious manifestations of that influence which Debussy was to find easier to absorb than to reject. But mostly, for all the Wagnerian textures of the piano part, the style of these songs is a mixed one (Ex. 3). This, the ending of 'Receuillement', shows some

interesting features. The harmony is largely triadic, but within a range of keys that the older professors at the Conservatoire perhaps found disturbing. The iambic rhythms of the piano part partially inhibit the forward flow of the music, so that the ear is concentrated rather on the moment, such as that in the second bar, where the low C natural bells pass through the B flat harmony. Finally, the melodic line captures the sense of the words with a precision of almost mathematical beauty, culminating in a phrase which, like many both in the songs and in *Pelléas*, looks far more tortuous than it sounds. The piano epilogue, from bar 8, returns to a more traditional melodic style in its emphasis on the 7th degree sounding over the tonic triad.

The Verlaine songs are also in a mixed style, but are generally less complex and more relaxed than the Baudelaire set. The opening of 'C'est l'extase' demonstrates a more reticent approach without any loss in expressive power (Ex. 4). It is a commonplace that Verlaine's poetry is among the most musical in the French language, and it seems that Debussy, responding to this, allowed the words to generate sounds in his imagination. The denser texture of Baudelaire's thought called forth not only denser musical textures but a conscious effort on the composer's part. One criticism of Ex. 4, as of the epilogue to 'Receuillement', might be of the rather routine piano echo in bars 9–10, but otherwise the

Ex.4

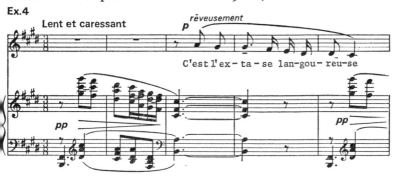

c'est là fa-tigue a-mour-eu - se.

blending of voice and piano is deftly managed, so that the phrase lengths are made up of six plus four bars, instead of the expected four plus four. Basically, these ten bars are a cadence from the dominant 9th to the tonic, but the 9th is so extended as to acquire a sound-value of its own. This process, here no doubt suggested by the words, soon became independent of textual bases. In bars 7–8 also, the accepted canons of harmonic progression are flouted by the repeating of a phrase as a self-contained entity.

The chord of the dominant major 9th held Debussy's affection throughout his life. He always seems to have found escape from it difficult and, from about 1888 onwards, even more than the dominant 7th, it begins to acquire a life of its own. In the last Baudelaire song, 'Le Jet d'Eau', written in 1889, the two chords of the ninth marked * are, if anything, the consonances upon which the preceding dissonances resolve (Ex. 5). This example also shows the importance that texture was already assuming in Debussy's music. The notion of a fountain suggests the pervading 5-note pattern; this is a perfectly orthodox response. But the actual noise of the water is uncannily reproduced by the placing and density of the left hand chords. The reader will find, if he tries out various dispositions of these notes, that Debussy's version has a magical conviction of its own.

Ex.5

En‑tre‑tient dou‑ce — ment l'ex‑ta — se   où ce soir m'a plon‑

‑gé l'a‑mour

La   ger — be   d'eau   qui   ber — ce ses mil‑le fleurs,

In the matter of form, the songs written before 1887 are too straightforward to need discussing, but in the Baudelaire songs—'Le Balcon' especially—the very length of the poems necessitates some formal planning: strophic treatment or endless melody are either irrelevant or impossible. In 'Harmonie du Soir' the complex *pantoum* verse form is followed in the music, a considerable feat of organisation. In 'Le Balcon', two phrases are developed in true Wagnerian fashion to provide almost all the musical material; further diversity is furnished by the alternation and superimposition of duple and triple rhythms and by changes of speed—in the 131 bars there are no fewer than 21 tempo markings. 'Le Jet d'eau' is a mine of organizational ingenuity, although on the surface the form could not be simpler: three verses with a repeated refrain. The setting of the refrain begins with a whole-tone chord which, while possibly expressive of 'la gerbe d'eau', has also a structural function in that its harmonically accommodating nature makes possible a smooth link between verse and refrain, no matter on what chord the verse ends. However, there is a distinct difference between verse and refrain in the style of the vocal writing. In contrast to the triplets and flexible prosody of the verse sections, where the weak quavers regularly anticipate the movement of the strong (see Ex. 5), the style of the refrains is more forceful, relying entirely on duple rhythms and firm accents at the beginning of each bar. By this means and by the characteristic whole-tone opening, the refrain is given in the music the uniqueness accorded to it in the poem, that is to say the traditionally clearer outline of the 'chorus' as opposed to that of the verse.

Over and above this, Debussy relates the first line of the first verse to the last line of the last refrain by repeating in syncopated movement the opening three notes of the vocal line; with this fragmented echo the music seems not to stop but to pass beyond our hearing. This idea of the spatial movement of sound, expressed not by physical grouping of instruments but by the material itself, can be traced from this song to its more sophisticated application in orchestral pieces such as *Nuages*, *Fêtes*, and *Gigues*.

The final sound of the song is of the major 2nds with which it began. Possibly Debussy got the idea of these from the music of Borodin; traces of Russian influence can be found in works of his as late as the *Nocturnes*. Whatever their source,

Debussy presents them here as a deliberate tonal enigma. Throughout the song they reappear as parts of traditional discords, dominant 7ths and major 9ths; only in the final bar do they come to rest as the 5th and 6th degrees over a firm major triad. From this we can see that tonality was one of Debussy's preoccupations at this time—an extended tonality certainly, but nevertheless a true one in the sense that control is exerted by certain key areas. Even in the chromatic welter of 'Le Balcon' the final C major tonality makes a monitory appearance a full 16 bars from the end, through which its effect is clearly felt. This, of course, is not to deny the growing importance of the sound-moment in Debussy's music of this period. The battle between these two principles continued to be fought for many years, and tonality proper is often obscured by modality in melody and harmony. As a way of escape from the established tonal system, modality offered a path just as viable as Wagnerian chromaticism and, for example, the Dorian opening of 'Il pleure dans mon cœur' from the Verlaine (*Ariettes oubliées*) set manages to convey much the same combination of simple expression and deep emotion that one finds in the poem (Ex. 6).

Ex.6

Modérément animé (triste et monotone)

pp con sordini

p un peu en dehors

All this indicates a composer with considerable technique at his command before his thirtieth year. But of piano and orchestral music these years provide hardly anything that sounds like the 'real' Debussy. The piano music in particular is remarkably jejune in both content and technical expression, whereas, as we have seen, in the songs the piano is treated as an equal with the singer and is made to produce some wonderful sounds. This difference is so strange as to suggest a psychological rather than a technical reason. Of all the dozen or so short piano pieces which appeared by 1891 only the famous *Clair de Lune* contains any hint of the way his piano writing would develop. The spacing of the opening thirds is a further exercise in those interdependent sonorities already seen in Ex. 5, while the C flat introduced into the reprise (bar 59) seems to tap some hidden source of energy in the instrument. The deployment of space is more assured in this piece than in any other before the suite *Pour le piano*; it is a rarity, a lollipop that is not all sugar and water.

The orchestral music—the suite *Printemps* and the *Fantaisie* for piano and orchestra—is also undistinguished, although pleasant and neatly put together. On a quite different level of invention is the *poème lyrique La Damoiselle élue*, on which Debussy worked from 1887–9. The journey from the sensuousness of Baudelaire and Verlaine to the conscious sublimity of Rossetti's *Blessed Damozel* may seem a long one. But it is closely comparable with that between the worlds of *Tristan* and *Parsifal*—Debussy heard *Parsifal* for the first time at Bayreuth in the summer of 1888. The influence of *Tristan* on Debussy was obvious and temporary; that of *Parsifal* both more subtle and more long-lasting. Over twenty years later he was to praise *Petrushka* for 'an orchestral infallibility that I have found only in *Parsifal*' and the blending of colours that Wagner achieved in this work was the principle of orchestration that Debussy followed from this time on.

So much can readily be heard. Less apparent is the extent to which Debussy borrowed for *La Damoiselle élue* some of the actual melodic shapes of Wagner's music drama, and from this point of view a comparison of the two orchestral preludes is most instructive. Both are built on three themes—*La*

Damoiselle in a clear 3-part structure, *Parsifal* in a more complex one—and the reader may judge for himself the similarities of theme (Ex. 7). The opening two bars of *La*

Ex.7

Damoiselle are indicative of the modal way of thinking into which Debussy readily fell when setting religious texts, but the orchestration of bars 3–4 accords very closely with that of bars 6–19 in *Parsifal*—decorative string arpeggios, pedal on the bottom, syncopated repeated notes in the middle, tune on the top. Furthermore, both opening sections die out on high, ethereal chords.

The differences between the works, however, are just as

marked. For every imitation of *Parsifal*, there are half-a-dozen textures which point to Debussy's later works—his use of the three trombones, for example. He uses them sparingly. At the climax of the whole work they play one 3-bar phrase, and apart from that their contribution is restricted to the repetition of a 2-bar phrase near the end and to 5 single, soft chords spaced throughout the work. In *Pelléas*, these instruments fulfil the same twin purposes, climactic and colouristic. The second is the one which takes our attention here. The 5 soft chords occur either at the beginning or at the end of sections, as a kind of textural punctuation, as though the grammar of the harmony were inadequate for the listener's orientation. Debussy uses their distinctive colour also in an attempt to reproduce an effect peculiar to the piano (Ex. 8). In his hands, the interaction of pianistic and

Ex.8

orchestral media was to become a fruitful source of new sounds: this particular combination of arco and pizzicato strings occurs frequently in later works.

The vocal writing is as different from Wagner's as could well be. The solo lines are already moving towards the kind of fluid arioso that came to perfection in *Pelléas*, but they tend still to be either plainly uninteresting or else broken up by intrusive passages of tunefulness, so that the overall effect is patchy. The writing for the women's chorus, however, because it sticks completely to a homophonic style and almost completely to triple rhythms, makes a considerable impact.

The harmonic style of these passages is also simple. Whether or not all this was the result of his enthusiasm for the works of Lassus, heard during his stay in Rome, the practical result is that the words of the chorus can actually be heard.

But quite the most astonishing sounds in the work come from the orchestra after the Damozel's final words (Ex. 9).

Ex.9

The bare fourths, the wide spacing, the tremolos, all depict the words—'the light thrilled towards her'—with sudden, overwhelming power. This dramatic passage, even if it breaks rather abruptly into the essentially cool ambience of the piece, gives a glimpse of the sounds orchestras were to be making early in the next century, in Debussy's own 'Jeux de vagues' from *La Mer*, or in the final section of Stravinsky's *Petrushka*.

Debussy had returned from Rome to Paris early in 1887. For him the next five years were years of hardship. For the first time he was thrown on his own resources, both financially and musically. There were no longer official grants to live on, no longer official attitudes to be defied. The piano music that emerged from this period consists largely of rewritings of earlier pieces, but even the new-minted works, with the one exception of *Clair de lune*, are as traditional as ever.

After finishing *Le Jet d'eau* in 1889, Debussy returned to song setting two years later and in 1892 produced the first of the triptychs that he was to favour from now on, the first series of *Fêtes galantes* to poems by Paul Verlaine. Even here, much of the material was old. The central song, 'Fantoches', dates

possibly from as much as ten years earlier. So does 'E
Sourdine', but Debussy reworked this song considerably
particularly its vocal line. The opening bars belong to hi
original conception, (Ex. 10) except that in the 4th bar of th

Ex.10

earlier version the B major chord returned with a predictabl
symmetry. In the later version quoted above, the fluidity o
the theme—the nightingale's song—is matched by that of th
harmony and the whole is in keeping with the markin

'rêveusement lent'. It is possible to see even from this short extract how the piano carries the melodic burden as well as providing atmosphere through texture and harmony. The voice is free to interpret the text, covering only a small range in the natural, unstressed rhythms of French speech: the gradual departure from an initial monotone, as well as being an echo of the nightingale's song, depicts graphically the opening words of the poem. This division of labour obtains throughout Debussy's output for this medium.

In the last song of the set, 'Clair de lune', Debussy abandoned an earlier version altogether and started afresh, and here for the first time we find the pentatonic scale in prominent use. Almost as it were in obedience to Saint-Saëns' prophecy, Debussy had been fascinated by the gamelan at the Paris Exhibition of 1889 and it was entirely typical of him that he should later use the sound not only imitatively, in a piece like *Pagodes*, but also in the String Quartet, in *La Mer*, and in this song where it is recreated to serve a different imaginative purpose (Ex. 11). Here the scale is based on F sharp, so that

Ex.11

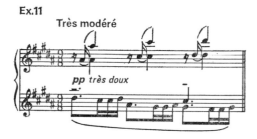

only the black notes of the piano are needed. The hands of the pianist-composer may have been responsible for this placing, but there is also no doubt that it makes it easier for the pianist to get the effect of '*pp*, très doux' which the composer and the text demand; the whole 4-bar introduction feels most peculiar if transposed.

It is worth looking at this song in more detail. The opening left-hand pattern is a sort of organizing motive for the whole song. Its compactness, in length and range, enables it to appear in every part of the keyboard without intruding unduly or disrupting the passage of the vocal line, and in many cases it exists entirely as a rhythmic idea. The three verses of the poem are set in a mixture of the strophic, the variational, and the free compositional manner. The opening of verse II is a reminder of verse I, no more. Verse III is quite new, although it incorporates the pattern of Ex. 11, and Debussy marks well the way in which 'au clair de lune' at the end of verse II is echoed by 'au calme clair de lune' at the beginning of verse III (Ex. 12). This echo is musically caught by the repetition of the rhythm, while the added-6th harmony anticipates the addition of the word 'calme'. We may notice also how the

Ex.12

Et leur chan-son se mêle au clair de lu — — ne,

Au cal — me clair de lu — ne tris-te et beau,

oxymoron 'triste at beau' is set well outside the tessitura of the preceding bar and how the second adjective is emphasized both by the shape of the vocal line and by the underlying harmony. The progression at this point is basically tonic-dominant; the continuation of the D sharp over both chords is typical of Debussy's harmonic style at this time. As we have seen, he preferred to adorn the perfect cadence with additional notes so that its cadential force would be softened. As a result, when he does use the perfect cadence plain, he does so for a purpose. In this song he uses it twice. First, to lead into verse II—this is purely a means of articulating the form—and secondly, to mark the final climax at the words 'et sangloter d'extase les jets d'eau', from which point the music slowly fades away. Perhaps the most remarkable thing about the song as a whole is the way in which the music catches the meaning of every word and phrase and still conveys the overall shape of the poem.

Church modes, Wagnerian chromaticism, Javanese gamelan music—such catholicity brought its own problems, and it is a mark of Debussy's genius not only that he was so clear in his own mind about the impasse into which traditional tonality had run, and, perhaps more importantly, traditional ideas about music in general, but that he was able to explore so many routes away from this impasse and still maintain an identity. It is surely natural that the finds of these journeys should be tried out first in short works such as these songs and we should not then be surprised that the 30-minute *L'Enfant prodigue*, written in 1884, was still his most extended work.

II

With the benefit of hindsight we may say that in *Fêtes galantes* Debussy had proved himself a mature composer, but only to the upper levels of French musical society was he a name that meant anything; Fauré had declared the Baudelaire songs to be the work of a genius, and quite apart from this the professors at the Conservatoire had good reason to remember his determined iconoclasm, but to the plain musical man in the streets of Paris the Debussy of 1892 was unknown. The performances of the String Quartet and of *Prélude à l'après-midi d'un faune*, in the Decembers of 1893 and 1894, changed all that.

For an audience going to hear a string quartet in 1893 in Paris the touchstone would have been the quartet by César Franck, first performed in that city 3 years earlier. Debussy too may have had Franck in mind, because the opening theme of his quartet undergoes a series of variations in the course of the work, in the 'cyclic' manner of many of Franck's compositions. Or, again, he may not. The principle of cyclic form is essentially the Germanic idea of development spread over a wider area. It may just as easily have reached Debussy from Schubert's 'Wanderer' Fantasia, from Liszt, or more likely Wagner, though obviously without the pictorial and psychological associations with which Wagner imbued it. Here is the opening theme, together with 7 of its later forms: (Ex. 13).

It can be seen from this that in the first 4 variations rhythm, tempo, and harmony were the main agents in Debussy's variation technique: the melodic outline stays very close to

x.13

a) **Animé et très décidé**

f

b)

p

un peu en dehors

(c) **Assez vif**

Viola

f

d) *p expressif*

pp

pp

pp

pizz.

e)

pp pizz.

sf

f) Vln. II

p.

(g) Très modéré   (h)

Cello

the original. These examples also provide a number of pointers to the direction in which Debussy's musical language was moving. The opening (Ex. 13a) is in the Phrygian mode but the descending pattern G–F sharp–F natural–E soon takes over, not as a modulating device but as an effect of colour inside the firm G minor tonality. The activity of the bass is noticeably sporadic, areas of movement contrasting with held pedals. Furthermore, when there is activity it is violent—such as the swift modulations in bar 5 from tentative F major to certain A flat major, achieved by purposeful movement in the bass. But even in such a vigorous passage the chords are all 7ths or 9ths. We may notice lastly how the long notes are placed in the middle of each bar. In this way the tonic accent is reduced, the music becomes fluid and nearer to Debussy's stated ideal of eternal improvisation. This fluidity applies also to the phrase structure: the first complete section is of 12 bars and it is possible to analyse the grouping as 2–3–4–3, although changes in the material occur so naturally that one could not argue against such an alternative as 2–2–3–3–2, but one may be firm in rejection of 4–4–4. This flexibility is not uncommon in Debussy's work, although on the other hand repetitions of 2-bar phrases also play a large part; for example, the song 'Green' is built entirely of such phrases and this is probably another instance of Russian influence. But such music is by no means as static as the mathematics suggest, because very often the material is arranged in the form ABAB¹, where B¹ gives rise to ideas for the succeeding bars.

(b) is remarkable alike for its weird texture and its atonal harmony. The arrival of a clear F sharp minor chord is felt as a vast relief. But the disruption in (c) is not so much tonal as textural and rhythmic. Here Debussy used altogether more boldly the combination of arco and pizzicato tried out in *La Damoiselle*. It is generally, and plausibly, considered that the germinal influence in this passage was the gamelan orchestra, although this time there is no sign of anything pentatonic. At any rate, the ostinato idea was to be a fruitful one, even in the simple form of accompaniment shown by (d). But in (e) the ostinato cello pattern is abandoned, the metre becomes 5 in a bar, and the harmony moves to a new triad on every beat. Essentially the movement is tonic—dominant—tonic, but the use of foreign root-position triads as steps in the progression is an important feature of Debussy's style, later to be found both in light-hearted pieces like *Minstrels* and *General Lavine* and in evocative ones like the study 'Pour les sonorités opposées'.

Not all the references to the original theme are as obvious as this: (f) borrows the triplet and the undulating outline, and that is all; while (g) alters the order of the first 4 notes, and the triplet becomes 6 semiquavers. In (h) the rhythmic pattern of (c) can be distinctly heard, but every other detail is new. The progressive dismemberment of the theme in the last movement makes the vigorous return of (e) all the more arresting.

With this work, Debussy shook the preconceptions of his contemporaries as to what a string quartet should sound like; with traditionally academic resources he produced quite unacademic sounds. In (d) the conception is really an orchestral one, rather in the style of the 'Forest Murmurs' from *Siegfried*, but the character which the theme here takes on is quite different from that of any birdsong or of anything in the quartet up to that moment; the composer marked it 'expressif', and one feels he might well have added 'mais en dehors'.

The attentive listener to this quartet will hear, apart from a lot of Debussy, touches of Grieg, Massenet, Wagner Franck, Borodin, the church modes, and the gamelan. The listener to *L'Après-midi* hears nothing but Debussy. The work which takes ten minutes to perform, took him two years to write and had probably been in his mind for long before that Perhaps as a result of this long gestation, one has the sense 'o something far more deeply interfused'. It was Debussy's firs masterpiece and it is pleasant to record that at the first performance it was enthusiastically encored, the only première of his to be so honoured. This is all the more remarkable because not only was the work revolutionary in its sounds and ideas, but to a large extent the sounds are the ideas, and the sounds, to judge from the account of one of Debussy's friends, were far from perfectly reproduced: 'the horns were appalling and the rest of the orchestra hardly much better.'

Apart from the flute, which is given a solo part, the instruments are brought together in ever new and fleeting amalgamations, and to analyse these is indeed to take a spade to a soufflé. The timing of entries, repetitions, and silences is quite unpredictable, and although there are two distinct themes in the work the overall effect is one of masterly discontinuity Debussy was trying not to reproduce Mallarmé's poem in music, but to decorate it, but even so the free association o. ideas is a technique common to both works. If in the quarte the art of composition sometimes shows through the surface in *L'Après-midi* the unity is apparently effortless.

The illusion of improvisation is, in a good performance easy for the listener to accept. Towards this end, all repetitions of material are in some way altered, in key, pitch harmony or orchestration, so that the two themes seem to grow from their experiences. Meanwhile, between the fuller appearances of the tunes, the tiny patterns on which they are built are shuffled and thrown together in new assemblies of

Ex. 14

(a)

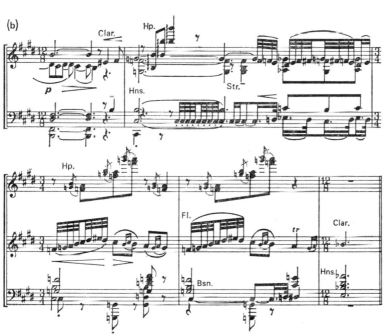

(b)

sound. Four bars from early in the work clearly demonstrate this process (Ex. 14b). After three attempts over various harmonies to prolong the ecstasy of the opening (a), for the first and only time until the final page the music reaches the dead-end of an unembellished root-position triad. The orchestra seems to take a deep breath and launch into something akin to a traditional development section. (a) is varied in a fairly straightforward manner on clarinet and flute, and the cellos play with an inversion of the theme, echoed in the final bar by the bassoon. But the sound of this passage is revolutionary, looking forward to the fragmented noises in *Jeux* nearly 20 years later. Spade in hand, we can perhaps dig up a few of the reasons.

In the second bar the horns play a sforzando chord, muted, the harp takes the bridging B natural and decorates it with octaves, the cellos stutter on C sharp before finding their fluency, 2nd violins and violas play an isolated dominant 7th. These four features are all effects of colour, serving no thematic purpose whatever, yet together they make up a large and indispensable part of the total sound. The other forward-looking feature is the use of the whole-tone scale in the last two bars. Already it has very nearly moved beyond the rôle of a linking passage, to which it was confined in his earlier works, to that of a basic sound, but Debussy was always alive to the danger of this scale becoming monotonous, and in any extended passage where it is used we can expect to find very clear rhythmic or textural articulation—here, the pizzicato string chords and appoggiaturas on the harp and the two melody instruments. Although the effects of colour are apparently random in their appearances, they operate on three distinct levels of texture—bass, central harmony, melody. This triple-layered sound is very common in Debussy's work, and in his piano music he eventually rationalized it by writing *La Puerta del Vino* on three staves. When writing for orchestra he was happily released from the restrictions of the human frame and could write long bass notes through changes in the harmony without considering any complications of pedalling. In *L'Après-midi* the bass hardly ever moves faster than a slow crotchet and this goes a long way towards creating the overall mood of sensuous enervation.

The years from this time until 1902 were spent mainly on two large-scale works, *Pelléas* and the *Nocturnes*. Of the *Nocturnes*, *Sirènes* gives the most compact demonstration of

Debussy's compositional principles. The female chorus is used as an orchestral effect, vocalizing in a manner as far different as can be imagined from the syllabic precision accorded to it in *La Damoiselle* (Ex. 15). These bars are,

Ex.15

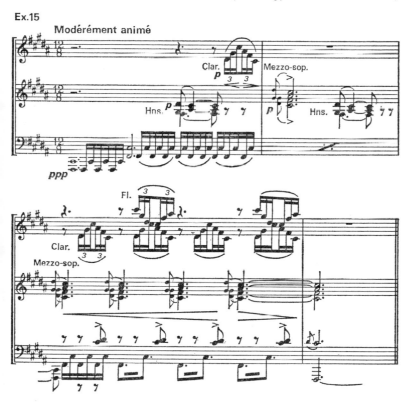

technically, no more than variations on the chord of F sharp major; the decorative techniques of *L'Après-midi* have been promoted to predominance, for not only have the singers no words, they have no tune either. This presents problems for singers brought up on more conventional music, and it must be admitted that even with the advantages of modern recording many choirs fail to convince the listener that the studio floor is a mysterious Mediterranean outcrop. Certainly Debussy would have found a more satisfactory medium in an age of synthesizers and white noise.

When the tune does appear it strikes a suitably exotic note—or rather two (Ex. 16). The sharpened 4th degree and the

Ex.16

Harmony: B♮7

flattened 7th, here only in the harmony, continue to be a favourite combination for the next decade—the horn theme from the first movement of *La Mer* is one of the most magical developments of this synthetic mode. These two themes also have in common their outline; initially they hesitate, explore the ground delineated by the opening, then gradually their confidence grows and they expand. Such quietly accommodating themes are common in Debussy's work, as opposed to the self-assertive themes to be found, for example, in Wagner's *Ring*. Did the idea perhaps come, again, from *Parsifal*, from the chorus of the flower maidens?

In the last example, the E sharp is something more than just exotic colouring because, together with the pedal B natural, it acts as the harmonic link between the theme and its repetition, albeit enharmonically disguised as F natural. This interval of the tritone between linking notes of an enharmonic progression is often also the interval at which a repeated melody is transposed, a distinctive method of treatment which Mussorgsky uses on the coronation theme in *Boris Godunov*. Mussorgsky plays up the opposition of pitches where Debussy handles it gently; very often, as here, a pedal note guides the transformation of the harmony.

The other two Nocturnes, *Nuages* and *Fêtes*, are musical paintings of Paris: in *Nuages*, cold under a grey sky, in *Fêtes*, bursting with democratic life. Both use themes in a more traditional way than *Sirènes* and both are brought to an end by a disintegration of their material. The art here lies largely in the timing of fragmented entries, and in particular in the timing of the silences between them. These 'silences' are not however complete, but are filled with imprecise noises, hardly appreciable as music: in *Nuages*, the rumble of the timpani, in *Fêtes* the scrubbing of cellos and basses, the rapping of a military drum, and one masterly tap on the cymbal (Ex. 17).

Ex. 17

After *L'Après-midi* and the *Nocturnes* it would be wide of the mark to say that Debussy's composing technique improved or matured. It simply changed in response either to the needs of the work in hand or, during the last ten years of his life, to the increasingly wry and melancholic view he began to take of life and of the part he had to play in it. The changes of style that we find in *Pelléas* can be explained well enough in terms of the new demands made by the setting of a prose

C

play. The eclectic Debussy had by now amassed most of the musical data that he was going to need for his life's work. He was fluent in his own language, his technique absolutely sure. The main interest of *Pelléas* lies, then, in the way he tackled the demands of the drama: the creation of distinct atmospheres, the handling of pace, the treatment in the vocal writing of passages that in the 19th century would have been set as recitative and aria, and especially the task of characterization. The choice of *Pelléas et Mélisande* was not that of a composer determined on worldly success. Fully three years before Debussy discovered the play of Maeterlinck, he gave a miraculously close description of it in his adumbration of what he would want from an ideal libretto, a grey dream-world sheltered from the shoutings of *verismo*. One must not imagine, however, that his deep involvement with the opera automatically solved the problems outlined above.

Two points of general harmonic interest have already been observed: that Debussy had an almost obsessive aversion to the unadorned perfect cadence and that, in *L'Après-midi*, he was beginning to use the whole-tone chord as a self-sufficient entity. In *Pelléas*, he found a use for the first and a whole range of uses for the second.

The perfect cadence had, since around 1600, been utilized as a final punctuation mark, bringing statements to a formal conclusion. For Debussy, music was not about statements. His ideal of improvisation implied rather a tuning-in to sounds already around us, and when the outward music stopped the inward music was still to be heard. *Ex cathedra* statements, 'This is the end', were not in his style, hence his fondness for fade-out endings and inconclusive conclusions. But, of course, in a dramatic work the pace and tension of scenes have to be graded with care. In some an atmosphere has to be established, in some the interest lies more in the give-and-take of the dialogue. Very simply, the atmosphere of this opera is one of distance, alienation, and mystery, as evoked by the modality and whole-tone harmony of the opening bars. Against this background, the perfect cadence retains its traditionally positive qualities, presenting an image of immediate presence or decisiveness, either mental or physical. Debussy is sparing in his use of it. Unadorned, it occurs fewer than 20 times in the whole opera, and in every single case the words or the character and emotions of the speaker provide an unambiguous reason (Ex. 18).

(a) shows a straightforward employment of the cadence. Arkel, the figure of experience and wisdom, encourages Mélisande to believe she is getting better—indeed he devotes half the opera's total of perfect cadences to this end. Note how the transition to the set of cadences passes through the doubt of a whole-tone chord; Arkel knows she is going to die. (b) is more subtle. Golaud is working up to his first, terrifying

Ex.18

(a)

(b) GOLAUD

On di-rait que les an-ges du ciel y cé-

Str. *p très doux*

-lè-brent sans ces-se un bap-tê - me.

Fl.

pp

(c) MÉLISANDE

Qu' al-lons nous fai-re main-te-nant?

Retenu

p

più p

PELLÉAS

Il ne faut pas s'in-quié-ter ain - si pour u - ne ba - gue.

a tempo

p

36

outburst of jealous rage. He looks into Mélisande's eyes and with the heaviest irony pronounces these words. Debussy matches the ironical text by the quasi-ecclesiastical chords and by orchestrating them all, except the last, for divisi strings after a passage dominated by harsh woodwind. The whole archaic effect is nicely capped by the perfect cadence; the success of irony at any time depends on precise diction, and here similarly on precise harmony. In (c) the music betrays the true feelings of Mélisande and Pelléas, their words notwithstanding. 'What are we going to do now?' asks Mélisande, who has carefully dropped her ring into the fountain by accident; the two perfect cadences give the lie to the helplessness of her question. 'You mustn't be so upset over a ring', replies Pelléas, but the minor-based Dorian mode freezes the comfort of his answer. It is the loss of this ring that sets the first spark to Golaud's evil temper, from which the whole tragedy springs.

By contrast, the whole-tone chord is used for its negative qualities. As it negates tonal harmony, so it destroys confidence and casts the shadow of doubt over bland assertions. In many cases it is associated with Golaud, whose jealousy, like Othello's, feeds on lack of proof. In the dungeon scene the whole of the orchestral part is based on the whole-tone scale, although Golaud and Pelléas sing notes outside it. As well as employing the usual syncopations and appoggiaturas, Debussy even fits a kind of tonal, ternary structure to this non-tonal scale by writing the outer sections in the C natural scale and the central section in the C sharp scale. But as he himself once said, quoting a passage from this scene, 'You'll admit no one could survive with those harmonies in his ears all day long'. Apart from this *tour de force* the whole-tone scale is presented in frequent, short passages in clear distinction to the chromatic, diatonic or modal harmonies that surround it (Ex. 19).

Ex.19

(a)

Animez un peu (sombre et inquiet)

Il y a quel-qu'un der-riè-re nous ....

Je ne vois per-son-ne .... J'ai en-ten-du du bruit...

Modéré

Je n'en-tends que ton coeur dans l'ob-scu-ri — té...J'ai en-ten-

-du cra-quer les feuil-les mor — tes ...

(b)

ARKEL

Mais la tris - tes - se,   Go-laud

Often, as in (a), it is combined with a low texture which reinforces its menacing qualities. Debussy introduces a further refinement in the first four bars, in that the music hesitates between whole-tone and diatonic harmony—between D natural and E flat—but as Mélisande's conviction of trouble grows, so the whole-tone chord establishes itself. The tonal bars, 7–9, reach a climax with a major 9th in bar 8 in an outburst which is distinctly a piece of old-style Debussy. In fact, he finished this scene, or a version of it, as early as 1893, but he may well have felt that the harmonies of the love duet should be left in their original state of innocence so that the whole-tone irruptions could strike with greater force. But perhaps the most imaginative juxtaposition of whole-tone and diatonic harmony occurs at the end of the opera (b). Arkel throughout has philosophized and dogmatized in tonal and modal harmony. Suddenly, his measured calm is shattered, and the harmony, instead of moving to the sane and reasonable C major that we expect, plunges into the doubt and horror of the whole-tone chord.

In the vocal writing of the opera Debussy exploited the styles already tested in the songs. The span of individual phrases is generally rather small, that is within a major 6th or minor 7th. This is exceeded in the more tempestuous and passionate moments, but even within such narrow limits

39

he was able to create a remarkably varied collection of declamatory styles by his exploitation of rhythm and harmony, and by his careful choice of the place where the singer moves off a given note (Ex. 20). Here we see three distinct vocal styles. Mélisande begins with a lyrical phrase over conventionally expressive harmony. Her line is made lyrical by the

Ex. 20

anticipation of the C sharp and D sharp on the weak quaver beats. Pelléas is disturbed by her inconsequential answers and the fast repeated notes mirror his agitation. Apart from the E natural the notes all change on the beat, as in the refrain of *Le Jet d'eau*, expressing the urgency of Pelléas' question, while at the same time the flexible rhythmic groups enable the singer to obey the marking 'serrez' in the idiom of French speech. Yet a third style is shown by Mélisande's answer. Here the voluptuous quality of her previous phrase is absent: the notes change on the beat. At the same time the rhythms are similarly straightforward and the style more declamatory than in Pelléas' *parlando* outburst. Elsewhere the vocal styles range from imitations of Massenet at the beginning of this love duet to distinctly awkward chromatic passages in Act III which rely on the harmony to give them coherence.

The last 3 bars of the previous extract mark the moment when the catastrophe begins. The castle gates are shut; Pelléas and Mélisande are trapped in the garden. The sound is a peculiarly evil one, not so much because of the whole-tone aggregations as because of the pitch and texture, so low and dense as to make the double-bass notes indeterminate. This is arguably not music but noise with a dramatic function and we can place it as a development of the sounds at the end of *Nuages* and *Fêtes*. The student who had shocked his fellows with a pianistic representation of the buses going down the Faubourg Poissonnière had found a more creative outlet for his mimetic abilities, and in doing so had out-Wagnered Wagner. The hammering of the Nibelung in *Rheingold*, probably the nearest Wagner ever came to the creation of pure noise, is still distinguished by the presence of a definite rhythm and by at least the memory of a melodic outline.

In the complex love-hate relationship between Debussy and Wagner, *Pelléas* is an act of homage and partial exorcism. A large proportion of the interludes actually sound like

Wagner and certainly they are quite different in effect from the body of the opera. Debussy wrote them in a hurry, as a practical necessity for the staging of the work, but it would be naïve to suppose that when pressed for time he could write only in a Wagnerian manner! As with the perfect cadence, in a dramatic work of this length no resource was beneath investigation and it is possible to argue not only that the Wagnerian, indeed Tristanesque, style is different from that of the sung part of the opera, but that it is different in a particularly relevant and dramatic way. The one principle, as opposed to technical detail, which Debussy took from Wagner was to let the orchestra explain the innuendos, the implications, and the interconnections of the story. The interludes were the only place where these factors could be discussed at length without the embarrassment of the actors' presence and of the need to accompany their communications; the only place where the misleading external impression of events could be examined for their true internal meaning. The choice of a distinct musical style for these deeper examinations was no more than sensible and by this choice Debussy was able to turn an unforeseen necessity into something that widens the impact of the opera (Ex. 21). Golaud and Mélisande are soon to arrive at the castle. Needless to say, there is nothing so crudely presented as an actual moment of arrival. Instead the interlude suggests the apprehension felt before a welcome of which one is not certain, and the music grows from the

Ex. 21

Plus modéré et très expressif

Animez et augmentez peu à peu

interplay of the two themes of Golaud and Mélisande. After hearing it, no one can doubt that Debussy was able to write meaningful counterpoint when he wanted to, whatever his strictures on 'academic' composition in general.

Finally we may examine the way in which he uses his themes. These, like Wagner's in the *Ring*, are themes both of people and of ideas. As one would expect, Debussy has left no explicit record of their references, which in some cases are deliberately wide and ambiguous—'to name a thing is to kill it.' But a distinct idea does accompany Golaud through the opera and, like the main theme of the Quartet, it is developed constantly (Ex. 22).

Ex. 22

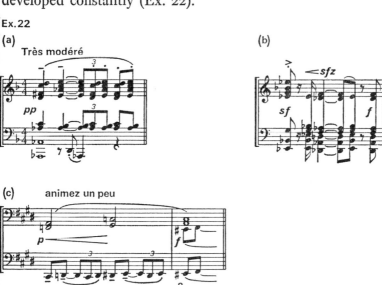

(a) is the first appearance of Golaud's theme. The syncopated rhythm with the long note in the middle of the bar, the
whole-tone harmony, and the obsessive repetition of two notes
—all these are recognizable components of Debussy's
general musical language, here synthesized with an alchemist's
care to symbolize Golaud's indecisive, uncontrolled, and
desperate nature. In (b) Golaud is ill in bed, but making light
of his injury, and his motive acquires a slightly self-conscious
vigour. (c) shows Golaud making his entrance in a cold fury;
the motive crawls chromatically up a fourth. After his fury
explodes, he storms out and the orchestra sums up in (d), the
motive now expanded to its utmost range of a tenth. But the
most intense expression of the motive is at the moment of
Pelléas's murder (e). The range here is compressed to a semi-
tone, in violent dissonance with the supporting harmony.
The C natural is stretched still further, the shape of the theme
altogether distorted. After the tragedy, (f) underlies Golaud's
final, inarticulate sobbing, and like Golaud the theme is
stripped of its power.

Even if Debussy made few innovations in his musical
language while writing this opera, it seems an inescapable
fact that he was forced to rationalize the resources he already
possessed. For an instinctive musician, such as he was,

44

this may well have been an irksome necessity, but it may in some part explain the firmer purpose to be heard in the music he wrote afterwards. In *L'Après-midi* he seems to have been guided by the light of his genius alone, which is why the work is so hard to analyse satisfactorily. In *La Mer* and the orchestral *Images*, partly no doubt because they are more extended works, there is more variety in pace, rhythm, and melody, a more conscious placing of section against section, brighter and harder orchestral colours, in all a greater sense of the dramatic. Without *Pelléas*, this change could hardly have come about so completely.

III

In the three years after the première of *Pelléas* Debussy reached his peak of productivity, and some would claim of inspiration also. A firmer purpose declares itself not only in the drive and energy of *La Mer* but in the sheer quantity of important, completed works: *La Mer*, two of the three *Estampes*, the first book of piano *Images*, *L'Isle joyeuse*, and a first, two-piano version of *Rondes de printemps* and *Ibéria*—all these were written in the years 1903–5.

But the purposeful style found in *La Mer* did not provide an entrée into the new world of piano music that Debussy now came to and conquered. In *Pour le piano* the final Toccata is purposeful enough, but the unrelenting figuration and text-book development of ideas place it firmly in the academic genre. There is none of the magic there that we find in, for example, *Pagodes*, the first of the three *Estampes*, published in 1903.

This magic—for want of a more objective word—seems at first to consist of a plain lack of purpose. The themes do not 'go' anywhere, the fingers stay for the most part obstinately on the black notes. From these melodic and harmonic points of view *Pagodes* may be thought of as one, extended pentatonic chord. But in other respects it shows a very clear purpose, particularly in the handling of rhythms, texture, and counterpoint (Ex. 23).

The opening bars (a), introduce the clash of major seconds and heavily syncopated rhythm which will serve as the background for a theme, to be played 'délicatement and presque sans nuances', that is, rather in the spirit of an

46

Ex.23

(a) Modérément animé

pp

2 Ped.

(b)

p

2 Ped.

(c) Sans lenteur

p

dans une sonorité plus claire

p

cresc.

ff

arabesque than of a full-blooded melody. A tenor counter-point is then added, to complete the progression from a single- to a four-layered texture. At (b) comes a break-back in this progression, to a free kind of three-part writing, in which the two upper parts are liberated from vertical considerations and produce ever-changing patterns out of the pentatonic series. The middle line is distinguished from the upper by its insistence on B natural, a note which the upper line avoids, while the spreading of the 3 parts over nearly 5 octaves sets this section apart from the more closely spaced chords of bar 3 onwards. The patterns continue to develop over a low pedal until the second idea (c) enters, in two layers contracted within the total span of a 9th. The characteristic sharpened 4th, here E sharp, breaks into the calculated monotony of the harmony, reinforcing the effect of the reduction in texture. As in the opening theme, the long notes come in the middle of the bar and this feature is a link with the variation of (b) which follows. Note how, in bar 5 of (c), the 3rd beat is left unstressed; with great effect it is then struck in the climax of bar 9. The full power of the four-beat bar is felt for the first time, although even here rising arabesques in bar 10 reduce the temperature. The second idea is then treated (d) in a contrasting manner of some complexity—if we count the left hand's G sharp as an intermittent pedal, there are again 4 layers—before the return of the opening idea. Significantly, the only change that Debussy makes at this important structural point is one of texture, letting the left hand down gently to its low pedal.

The next 19 bars are an exact repeat of bars 3–21; this represents nearly a fifth of the total length of the piece, a larger proportion of straight repetition than he was to allow himself in any succeeding piano work except *Mouvement*. Possibly he was aiming in *Pagodes* at a kind of ritualistic insistence of sounds. In the coda he reviews some of the main melodic ideas of the piece, fitting them in as the middle of 3 layers of sound, between low pedal notes and high arpeggios. In this way they are stripped of their original power and given an impersonal conformity which, while far from perfunctory or dull, balances the neutral atmosphere in which the work began. The final bars at (e) show the climax of (c) distilled into a single chord.

In all these examples texture is the composer's predominant concern, and it is a new use of vertical space in the writing that produces the 'magical' effect. This style owes much to Ravel's *Jeux d'eau*, published in 1901, as we can see by comparing the coda of this work with that of *Pagodes*, but there is really no question of plagiarism; Ravel's work may have suggested to Debussy some of the possibilities of a new technique, but Debussy realized them in his own way. The two works mentioned end with the markings 'sans ralentir' (*Jeux d'eau*) and 'retenu' (*Pagodes*). Ravel's mechanical fountain stops; Debussy's pagodas fade on the sight of the departing traveller.

Debussy further explored this style—'the technique of

illusion', as Edward Lockspeiser has called it—in the first set of *Images*. 'The first piece doesn't satisfy me at all', he wrote to his publisher in August 1905, 'so I've made up my mind to write another one, using different ideas and the most recent discoveries of harmonic chemistry.' Reading behind his defensive irony, we may surmise that at that stage all was not well. However, three weeks later he wrote again: 'without false vanity, I think these three pieces hold together and will take their place in the literature of the piano. . . . to the left of Schumann or to the right of Chopin . . . ' Whatever the stresses of composition, it is possible to trace in the first piece, *Reflets dans l'eau*, a development from the style of *Pagodes*, particularly in form and in originality of sound.

As in the earlier piece, there are recognizable patterns, too short to be called themes, which pervade the texture and through which, on the last page, Debussy conveys the impression of a return to the beginning of the piece. But it is little more than an impression, certainly no straight repetition of a whole paragraph, and the way in which the return is prepared shows a different approach to the problem from that in *Pagodes*, where the very idea of preparation is alien to the mosaic nature of the structure (Ex. 24). In (a) the shape of each 3-note pattern in the right hand is that of a wave; so is the shape of each 2-bar phrase. The three isolated left-hand notes stand out from this, but at the same time they are

Ex.24
(a)

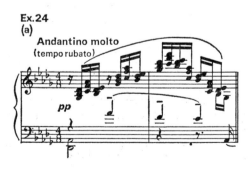

(b)

pp doux et expressif

rhythmically an augmentation of the right hand's 3-note patterns. The pedal supports the whole structure, reinforcing the left hand phrase with its harmonics—A flat and F natural by the D flat, E flat by the A flat. The right hand chords receive varying degrees of support from the bass, but the interesting thing about them is that the three chords are rhythmically shifted in the 2nd bar, producing a pleasing asymmetry. All this takes place inside a clear D flat major tonality. Thus far, at least, the remark about 'harmonic chemistry' appears purely ironic.

The second germinal phrase in the piece, (b), begins with a wave shape but curls back up to a foreign note, suggesting a change of harmony and possibilities of dramatic development which are taken up at a later stage; for the moment, though, expansionist tendencies are suppressed. In preparation for the reprise, Debussy combines (a) and (b) with unassuming skill (Ex. 25). The first attempt is stalemated in bar 3 by a plain C minor chord. The second attempt reaches the more fertile plains of a major 9th on A flat, from which point the mechanics of returning to D flat major could not be easier; the skill lies in the timing of the operation and in the exploitation of those melodic and rhythmic factors common

Ex. 25

pp

to (a) and (b). The rhythm of the upper part is slowed down
to three triplets and in bars 11 and 12 its movement is stilled
by the all-important 3-note pattern of the lower part, both
signs that the end is at hand. Finally, we may appreciate the
delicacy with which Debussy, having D flat major at his
mercy, delays for four bars its confirmation by the bass notes

Within the clear D flat tonality there is at least one passage
of harmonic interest, in the 13 bars before the main climax of
the piece. Under the marking 'en animant' the left hand
climbs two octaves through the whole-tone scale, while
the right hand alternates between minor and augmented
triads. The whole-tone harmony takes over briefly, before

chords of the 9th and 7th lead to a climax on an E flat triad. This opposition of tonal and non-tonal forces is entirely successful in giving a sense of forward movement to the whole paragraph, and is a quite logical extension of the treatment of the perfect cadence in *Pelléas*, applied here not to two chords but to one; for, apart from the final bar, this climactic one is the only one in the piece filled by an unambiguous major triad.

The climax is a powerful one in which (b), so far suppressed or fragmented, is given a chance to flower over stable harmonies, but even so the moment passes in a mere 5 bars of full volume, in a piece 95 bars long. This distrust of rhetoric shows also in the extract from the second letter above, where a high-sounding reference to the 'literature of the piano' prompts him to instant deflationary measures. After this climax the last 33 bars are an almost continuous diminuendo—the ripples after the splash—and the finality of the last chord is achieved not only by the harmonic means of a major triad but by the very wide spacing of it, which, but for the low C natural in Ex. 25, enfolds the range of the whole piece. The temptation to continue the metaphor of the ripples at this point is strong. Debussy himself detested the word 'impressionism' and would claim with Beethoven that this piece was 'more an expression of feeling than painting'; nevertheless, it is incontestable that there are some physical affinities between this piece and the actual behaviour of reflections in water. The 'wave' patterns themselves and the distorted likenesses between them are two obvious examples. But we can readily forgive the magician for protesting when some of his audience imply that the sum total of his art consists in the manipulation of a box of tricks.

One of the most original passages in the piece again approaches the border between sound and noise (Ex. 26). After a cascade of pentatonic harmony the major 2nds provide a moment of colour—we may compare this with

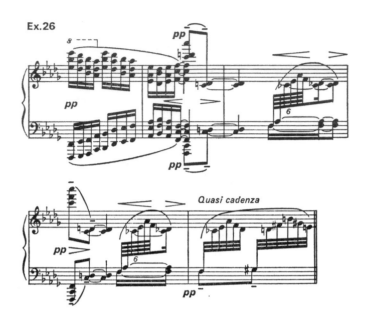

Ex.26

their more traditional, accompanimental use in a previous water piece, *Le Jet d'eau*. They are answered by a phrase of the wave pattern outlined in the first bar, and the two ideas are simply joined by the F natural which supports them both. As often, it takes two attempts to shift this reluctant bass, here through the development of the wave pattern in rising sequence. The impetus for this development comes from the diminishing note values in both the phrases, anticipating the 'stringendo' marking by a built-in accelerando. This is a good example of how Debussy's music can be at once static and dynamic; the short-long note rhythms reduce the linear flow but at the same time the overall tempo is increased until the music bursts from its static confines. Finally, we may well admire the economy with which the 'quasi cadenza' figuration is naturally developed into accompanying figuration for Ex. 24b. Altogether, the coherence of this piece is less a matter of controlled monotony, as in *Pagodes*, and more one of organic development and the assimilation of all themes into a wave pattern. This new-found predominance of shape over interval is crucial to his later style, culminating in the use of similar wave patterns in *Jeux*. Was this what he meant by 'using different ideas'? At any rate, the 'harmonic chemistry' seems to have been a blind. Not even a sympathetic editor was to be let completely into the magician's secrets.

Even if *Pagodes* and *Reflets dans l'eau* do not sound 'purposeful', for the first time outside song Debussy had turned the solo piano to his own purposes. He was the master, but his triumph was celebrated in private, for those who had ears to hear. In *L'Isle joyeuse*, however, and in *La Mer* he put on a public face for the first time since the composition of *Fêtes*.

The opening of *L'Isle joyeuse* has obvious affinities with that of *L'Après-midi* in the way that it oscillates between C sharp and G natural, (Ex. 27), but the arabesque is far bolder, and

Ex. 27

on the piano it is impossible not to play it with a slightly percussive quality. The whole-tone elements are employed not for the purpose of dreamy apostrophizing but as aids to repressing the tonality until the 7th bar. This chord is given a more positive rôle in the final bars, which present the initial idea in a more formal manner (Ex. 28). Note the culminating

Ex. 28

synthesis of two themes, as in *Reflets dans l'eau*, the driving force of the repetitions, the prominent sharpened 4th, and the flourish of the final 2 bars, which encompasses the range not only of the piece but of an 85-note keyboard.

In *La Mer*, too, the whole-tone harmony is often partnered by vigorous rhythms, while all the other resources of Debussy's language go towards making this work one of his richest and most varied. The opening bars, evocative of dawn (Ex. 29), show a more refined, complex use of the

Ex 29

pentatonic scale even than that of *Pagodes*—one can almost hear Debussy's ironic comment, 'And doesn't the sun rise in the East?' Two passages in particular, from *La Mer* and *L'Isle joyeuse*, show a remarkably similar mood of buoyancy and confidence, unlike anything heard so far in his music;

Ex. 30

(a) Très rhythmé

(b)

the brass band in *Fêtes* is, in a sense, not Debussy but a happening which he incorporated into his score, whereas these two examples grow out of the preceding material (Ex. 30). Again the wave pattern is the guiding outline, but in addition to this both are boldly diatonic and move to the same springy rhythm. The long note is in the middle once more, but there is no feeling of enervation. Apollo has given way to Dionysus. Further similarities between these two works are easy to find— the whole-tone scale in passages of development, the synthetic mode with sharpened 4th and flattened 7th, and real tunes instead of pregnant phrases. Also, both works end with a bang. But, viewed as part of his total output, the outer movements of *La Mer* and *L'Isle joyeuse* figure rather as rogue specimens. More representative and, for a study of Debussy's later style, more interesting is the central movement of *La Mer*, 'Jeux de vagues'.

Pierre Boulez has approved this movement for its 'bold and radical conception of timbre', its 'elegant, condensed, and elliptical syntax'. Naturally, these are qualities that a composer like Boulez would admire, but many would agree with his implicit comment that the movement is remarkable not only for possessing these qualities but for possessing them to such a degree at such a period in musical history. It is difficult to convey elegance of syntax with one short example, but the following extract will give some idea at least of the qualities that Boulez admires (Ex. 31).

Ex. 31

59

The relevance of the clarinet's entry in bar 5 is easier to hear than to analyse, although the 4 descending notes are obviously derived from the ostinato figure. But apart from this, a casual look reveals nothing more than a multiplicity of patterns darting and weaving across the page. In this thematic wilderness even the tiny horn phrase in bar 6 sounds significant—but of what? Have the motivic procedures of the String Quartet and of *Pelléas* been so refined as to evade almost completely the clumsy investigations of the human intellect? The phrase sounds right, and that, Debussy would insist, is enough. But if we look at such passages from the point of view of their texture, the density of chords, the characteristic melodic and rhythmic shapes of certain instrumental groups, then the technique becomes clearer. Let us, for example, consider the horn parts of these same ten bars (Ex. 32).

Ex. 32

The phrases are clearly unified, either by melody or by rhythm. They are the centre round which the other parts revolve, as the instruments change partners, take up the ostinato at different points or add single touches of colour. In opposition to the solid textural identity of the horns stands the melodic identity of the ostinato, given primarily to violins and flutes but supported also at various times by oboes, clarinets, bassoons, cor anglais, violas, cellos, and harp. To return now to the question of the relevance and rightness of the clarinet entry, we can see that, after the initial D natural, it comprises the 4-note ostinato followed by a variation of the 3-note pattern in the horn part. But this, while a possible clue to its thematic relevance, gives at best a partial explanation of its rightness. One thing is certain: the orchestral colours are vital to the sense. Although Debussy made a four-hand piano version of the whole work, this movement is the least rewarding of the three to play in this manner, and the whole work in its turn less rewarding than a rendering of the vocal score of *Pelléas* by voice and piano. In short, he was beginning to escape from his fingers.

At the same time as his orchestral writing began to lose contact with the pianistic medium, so his piano writing became more orchestral. As one would expect, the use of colour as an organizing element came to him through writing for the orchestra. His 'orchestral' piano writing is simply an extension of this principle. Of course, colour on the piano is more nearly tied to pitch and texture and can be quite different from that produced by an orchestra playing the same notes. With this use of colour as a characteristic of the middle period piano pieces goes a separation of strands of sound, a counterpoint not so much of themes as of sound-worlds.

The similarities and differences between Debussy's styles in the two media can be illustrated from the following pair of examples, taken from *Poissons d'or*, the third of the second set of *Images*, written in 1907–8, and from *Pelléas* (Ex. 33). The idea of water is common to both. In (b) the luminosity of the piano texture is recreated in orchestral terms by reinforcing a woodwind sound with a percussive one; oboes with harp, flutes with plucked strings. The whole is bound together by a solo horn, taking the place of the left hand trill. The necessary differences between the media can be gauged if we think how equally unsatisfactory we should find a plain dotted minim in the piano left hand and a trill on the horn. The last two bars of (a) show more clearly the application of

Ex. 33

(a)

(b)

orchestral principles to the piano writing. It is 'scored' for two piano noises, a confused burbling and a theme in thirds. The confusion is suggested by the carefully pitched ambiguity of G double sharp against A sharp in the tenor register. Placed much higher, the dissonance would lose this ambiguity, and when it is in fact transposed a fifth down it already sounds dangerously gruff. The theme over it is enabled to stand out by virtue of the peculiarly percussive resonance produced by playing it 'détaché' with a half-pedal.

An equally clear example of orchestral technique brought to bear on piano writing comes from the first piece in the same set, *Cloches à travers les feuilles* (Ex. 34). The three layers of

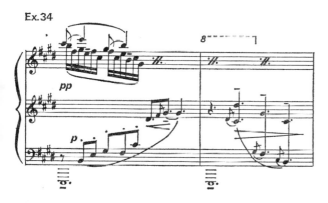

Ex. 34

the writing are clearly separated, more clearly than in *Pagodes*, and, as often, such melodic interest as there is lies in the middle part, over a bass pedal and under a fast repeated pattern high in the right hand. But the interesting point is the different dynamic treatment of this central line, starting louder than the others and becoming louder still before returning to their level. From a practical point of view, it is surprisingly hard to keep the right hand at a uniform pianissimo during this crescendo in the left, but this is clearly the effect intended, reproducing in pianistic terms the shifting colours of Ex. 31 from 'Jeux de vagues'.

The *Images* for orchestra might seem an obvious parallel to consider beside those for the piano, but they in fact show a change of emphasis, both from the homonymous piano pieces and from *La Mer*. In *Gigues* and *Rondes de printemps* the speech is less direct than in *La Mer*, the tone of voice less seductive than in *L'Après-midi*. Debussy's contemporaries registered disappointment and scorn in accordance with their previous sympathies, and the strange, half-lit world that these movements evoke has never appealed to more than a specialized audience. In retrospect we can see that Debussy was moving towards the more sophisticated syntax and orchestration of *Jeux* and it is arguable that the oboe d'amore tune in *Gigues*, lovely though it may be, is too imposing for the structure that contains it and that the interplay between it and the 'Keel Row' produces bewilderment rather than variety or tension. Certainly, the 'Keel Row' itself is not such stuff as climaxes are made on and Debussy's attempt is ill-fated. In *Rondes de printemps* the song 'Nous n'irons plus au bois' lends itself better to such emphatic treatment. Apart from this, the tune had haunted Debussy for at least 25 years —this was the third time he quoted it in his music—and he had had time to form an accurate idea of its possibilities. The more reflective moments in *Rondes* are often ravishing, yet the work as a whole lacks the fine but indestructible thread of logic that binds *L'Après-midi* or *Jeux*. In *Ibéria*, on the other hand, Debussy was stimulated by the strong, distinctive rhythms, harmonies, and colours of Spanish music, and it was his most ambitious working of the vein explored already in *Mandoline* and *Soirée dans Grenade*. This exploitation of things Spanish is in itself nothing unusual in a French composer of that period. Altogether more interesting is a kind of interruption that seems to stem from a peculiarly naïve, dramatic view that Debussy took of 'la vie espagnole'; it occurs in both *Soirée dans Grenade* and the transition from the 2nd to the 3rd movement of *Ibéria* (Ex. 35). In the piano piece it is an interruption that comes twice and then passes; in *Ibéria* the interruption at the third attempt proves to be the music of the last movement which, with Mediterranean impatience, has got tired of waiting. The result is not far removed from the indiscretions of a Charles Ives brass band,

Soirée dans Grenade

but it is an idea perfectly consistent with Debussy's notion of music as improvised sound. We can trace this interruptive technique back to *Pelléas*, Act IV scene 4, (Ex. 19a), where the love music and Golaud's music are similarly interlocked, but in the two later examples there is no dramatic justification and the juxtaposition is much tighter.

Ibéria, finished on Christmas Day 1908, was Debussy's last major effort of extroversion. Increasingly his music now turned inwards, and for the third time in his career it was a writer who provided the motivating force—after Verlaine

E

and Maeterlinck, the 15th-century poet and profligate, François Villon. And as in the *Ariettes oubliées* and *Pelléas*, this association produced new styles of music in combination with the old.

IV

These new styles arose largely from the nature of the poetry. As in the settings of Charles d'Orléans he had made some years earlier, the medieval text itself provided a pretext for simplicity of texture and harmony, but in the *Trois Ballades de François Villon* the immediacy of the emotions expressed forces itself through the surface of the pastiche. In the first two poems the poet's feelings are deep and expressed explicitly, in contrast to Verlaine's allusive, symbolic approach. How far Debussy chose the poems for this quality of directness it is impossible to say, but he in turn wrote direct music, condensing the irony and bitterness of a Golaud into the simplest of musical material (Ex. 36).

In this example from the first song time is noticeably treated as something fluid, not only through the markings 'en animant', 'retenu', and 'serrez', but also through the hysterical acceleration of the piano's 'laughing' pattern in bar 2. The piano's silence in bars 3 and 4 is more expressive than any notes could be of the poet's disrupted personality, of the frightening alternations between his hilarity and his despair. Together with these progressive features we find one reminiscent of his earlier years, in that the opening phrase of this first song recurs no fewer than 6 times in the Aeolian mode on F sharp, leading eventually to a cadence on F sharp major. There is a remarkably strong return to modality in many of his later works, by means of which he was able to evade the clutches both of Wagnerian chromaticism and of the tonal cliché. In some sense also, the pressure of the poet's and composer's emotion shows more clearly when encased in such

Ex.36

a conventional strophic form and expressed in such simple language. The second song, a prayer to the Virgin, uses modality more consciously as an archaic device, and with this modality goes a flexible use of triads, conveying the archaic effect without the tonal restrictions of the true 'stile antico'. This technique has been commented on often enough as one of the means by which Debussy extended tonality, but just as noteworthy is the variety of effects he obtained with it: in the prelude *General Lavine* a distortion of trumpet calls with parodying intent, in this prayer of Villon true religious devotion, and a rather more exotic kind of mysticism at the opening of *Le Martyre de Saint Sébastien* (Ex. 37).

Ex.37

(a)

General Lavine

(b)

Prayer to the Virgin

Pa-ra-dis painct où sont har- pes et

luz, Et ung en-fer où dam-nez sont boul – luz.

(c)

Saint Sébastien

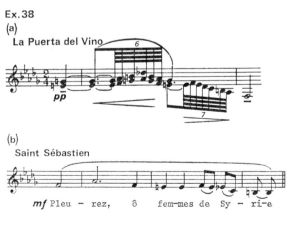

Le Martyre, a mystery in five acts to a text by d'Annunzio, is a strange and disturbing work. It displays, for one thing, such a variety of musical styles and levels of inspiration. The variety of language is probably larger than in any other of Debussy's works, and from this point onwards he became increasingly selective in the type of material he used for any one work. Partly, as in *Pelléas*, this variety is a concomitant of the work's length, but naturally some of the new ideas are suggested by the text, although he seems to have regarded such 'gapped' scales as belonging equally to Spain and the Near East (Ex. 38). The uneven level of inspiration may be attributable simply to the necessary speed of composition, but apart from that it is hard to imagine that the muscular Christianity of Psalm 150 really appealed to him, and the brass fanfares

Ex. 38

(a)

La Puerta del Vino

(b)

Saint Sébastien

mf Pleu — rez, ô fem-mes de Sy — ri-e

for the council of false gods can sound dangerously like some provincial embellishment to *Aladdin*. Debussy did not here solve the difficulty of writing bad music well, but the final psalm, which is meant to be 'good' music in both senses of the word, is little short of banal. It was rumoured at the time of the first performance in 1911 that this chorus was completely the work of André Caplet, who certainly helped with the orchestration of Debussy's sketches; we shall probably never know the truth, but even if such a proof were possible it would exonerate his musicianship only at the expense of his integrity. The remark Debussy later made to Koechlin about his Egyptian ballet for Maud Allan, 'Write *Khamma* yourself and I will sign it', may plausibly be attributed to a sick man's temporary irritability. His imagination was still responsive to concrete images, as we can hear from Sébastien's dance on the red-hot coals, where the sonorities of *La Mer* are power-fully recreated without any of the firm thematic bases of the earlier work.

Indeed, from this time Debussy seems to have outgrown dependence on themes, even in the restricted sense in which the word can be used about his particular kind of brief pattern, though of course he still used them when he wanted to. But in *Jeux*, for example, the ideas are self-generating, and no melodic line remains the same twice. The control of structure is exerted by the wave pattern to which, as Herbert Eimert has pointed out, all the ideas conform. We may trace a correspondence between this shape, returning on itself, and Debussy's very frequent ternary form, found especially in his shorter works. Where his style has often been called 'static' it might be truer to call it 'obsessive', in that movement does occur, but within the control of the dominant idea. *Jeux* represents Debussy's most whole-hearted develop-ment of this technique, already outlined in *Reflets dans l'eau*. Another technique for which *Jeux* provides an extreme example is the premature termination of a climax, again fore-shadowed in *Reflets dans l'eau* and further developed in Ex. 36 (Ex. 39). The pretext of the scenario—the three characters dance and one of the girls suddenly feels neglected—does not detract from the musical originality of this passage, in particular the disjointed falling patterns of the last 3 bars.

Ex. 39

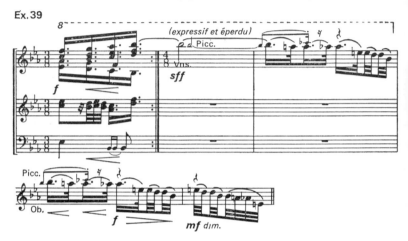

Quite apart from these details of grammar and syntax, *Jeux* was a milestone in Debussy's development. The eye, fixed on the score, can still pick out the 4-bar phrases, the tritonal relationships, the consecutive triads in root position, but the ear is continually being surprised and seduced by the sound of it all. A debt is clearly owed here to Stravinsky's *Petrushka*, in the frequent use of heterophony and especially in the intermingling of mystery with vulgarity. The give-and-take of the game of tennis is enacted in the orchestra as well as on the stage: a vulgar forehand drive from the string section is deftly turned by a mysterious lob from the solo flute. Often there seem to be several games going on at once, as in the passage of recovery from the main climax of the work (Ex. 40). Like a conjurer, Debussy sometimes tries to distract us from the mechanics of the show by making decorative and

Ex. 40 Très modéré

ultimately irrelevant gestures, but he has the technique to compel our attention when he needs to. The 140 bars that lead up to the main climax are as compelling as anything he ever wrote, and it is entirely characteristic that half-way through this build-up he should abandon the wide, swinging theme, reminiscent of the Franckian 'song of the sea' in the last movement of *La Mer*, and construct the remaining 70 bars out of two simple patterns, of 3 and 4 notes. Altogether, *Jeux* was a prophetic work, in the way it used colour as a primary element and in its freedom from any predetermined form. Even the orthodox-looking 8-bar frame is finally invaded by material from the picture itself.

The selection he made from the pool of styles in *Le Martyre* was a wide one. The whole-tone harmony, in which *Le Martyre* is rich, envelops the structure of *Jeux* and is treated as basic material in the piano prelude *Voiles*; the pentatonic

F

harmony of Erigone's solo comes again in the last movement of the Sonata for flute, viola, and harp, the modality of the opening bars (Ex. 37) in the cello sonata, and the rhythmic drive of Sébastien's dance with just as great effect in *En Blanc et Noir* and in the study 'Pour les accords'. But within the individual works, and the individual movements, the styles are more narrowly confined. It seems almost that in *Le Martyre* Debussy's language had grown too diffuse and that now he began to ration himself. This rationing process may not have taken place consciously, but it is noteworthy that the *Études*, in which particular styles of writing are suggested by the technical limitations, are far more successful than the second set of *Préludes*. As in the case of modality in the Villon songs, this very concentration of language produced some powerful music.

It should not be necessary to stress, nowadays, that Debussy's music is often powerful and not just moonlight and waterfalls or even, as Graham Greene once described it, 'cool, professorial music'. But actual violence is rarely found in it and is usually associated with natural forces. In *Pelléas*, the violence of Golaud is a dramatic necessity, but one of the points of the opera is that Golaud is not generally a violent character, it is just that there is a violent streak in him which he cannot control. The music that Debussy writes for him gains conviction from the fact that his music in general is not like that. As an example of the depiction of violence in nature we may take the opening of the 3rd movement of *La Mer*, where the sound is conceived orchestrally. A similar image in the piano prelude *Ce qu' a vu le vent d'ouest* is conveyed with more terrifying force because of the restrictions of the medium. The power of the 'wild, west wind' is conjured up by cascades of annihilating major 2nds, sounding very different from the major 2nds in *Le Jet d'Eau* 25 years before. They occur again in the middle movement of *En Blanc et*

Noir where, in an evocation of the horrors of war, their evil clatter accompanies the blaring chorale 'Ein feste Burg'. But 'accompanies' is the wrong word. It is a confrontation between the tonal chorale and the atonal 2nds, and the effect of dissociation is all the more terrifying because both effects proceed independently with the utmost confidence.

The ultimate in exploitation of dissociated material lies in bi-and polytonality. Debussy never used these techniques as a permanent basis for his music, as Milhaud and Koechlin were doing at about this time, but for special effects bitonality sometimes reinforces the spatial difference between layers of the texture. In other words, interruptions like those in *Soirée dans Grenade* and *Ibéria* now sound simultaneously with the prevailing material. A particularly successful example may be taken from the prelude *Feux d'artifice* where what is almost the French equivalent of Luther's chorale—the *Marseillaise*—is heard in the 'distance' (Ex. 41).

This passage shows also that Debussy's composing technique retained much that was familiar in spite of explorations in the territory of new noises. The rising 5th in the opening bar is expanded, gently at first, then with increasing abandon, until in the 4th bar the three levels of the keyboard join in a chorus of rejoicing. In the work of a more orthodox, 19th-century composer the excitement thus generated would

Ex. 41

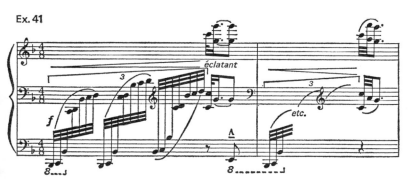

probably be dispersed in an expansive tune but, as in *Jeux*, Debussy has already made enough grand gestures and the whole affair is dismissed in the double glissando, literally brushed aside. The glissando itself gives rise to a few uneasy echoes and our ears are prepared for the coming alienation of sound sources by the final echo in bars 9–10; this allows the low tremolando only a gradual take-over and anticipates the initial downward shape of the *Marseillaise* fragment. It is instructive now to look back at bars 4 and 5 and see how naturally the rising 5th has been developed into sequences of three descending notes, also in preparation for the *Marseillaise* entry. This kind of backwards composing is obviously only necessary when the composer is working towards a given passage of music—as in the case of a classical symphonist approaching the recapitulation—but Debussy's skill at doing so should make one at least a little less dogmatic about his addiction to generative techniques.

This passage is interesting also from the point of view of its sound, in the way that the clean, hard sound of the major 2nds in the first two bars resolves into the intentionally brash, vulgar minor 9ths in bars 4–5. The resolution is so swift that the vulgarity is on us before we can escape, and this lack of proportion is reflected in the equally swift dismissal of bar 6. This is harmony used for what must be called textural rather than tonal purposes: the exact pitch of the minor 9ths is decided by the extent of the development in bar 3 and is quite irrelevant to the making of the harmonic contrast.

The *Marseillaise* extract is marked 'de très loin'. If we accept that it sounds so without much effort on the pianist's part, we may ask why. Partly it is the bitonality, partly the distance from the left-hand tremolo. But a further reason is the phrase's very familiarity and tunefulness, in a texture otherwise composed of small fragments in ever-shifting positions and shapes. As in the case of the Luther chorale in *En Blanc et Noir*, it sounds foreign because of its associations with tonal harmony and its resulting dynamic shape.

It is likely that Debussy's avoidance of tunes, in some of the music he wrote around 1911–13, was due to the difficulties in reconciling them with his intricate structural procedures. A preoccupation with patterns rather than with melodies in the accepted sense is evident in much of his music from as early as the *Ariettes oubliées*, but the patterns, though short, always developed into something singable, as in the climax to *Reflets dans l'eau*, which otherwise does not lend itself to vocal performance. In *Jeux*, however, the fragmentation is continual and in some of the *Études* this process reaches its climax. Of course, studies are not meant to be sung, but even in the most abstract of those by Chopin there is a melodic thread in the texture which one can follow. The development in Debussy's thinking on this point may be gauged by comparing passages from two 'moto perpetuo' pieces, *Mouvement* from the first set of 'Images' (1905) and *Pour les huit doigts* (1915) (Ex. 42).

These passages are the clearest exposition of melodic material in their respective works. The difference between these expositions in the matter of tunefulness is plain enough, and it is emphasized by the relative frequencies of melodic material in the two pieces. In *Mouvement*, well over half the bars contain what is, by any standard, melodic material; that is, it is possible to sing it in such a way that it can be recog-

Ex. 42

(a)

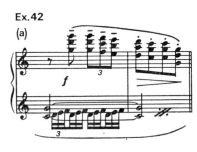

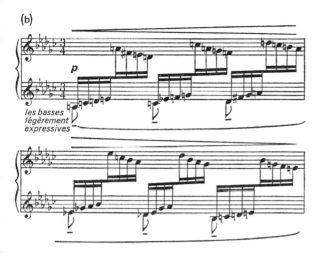

(b)

les basses légèrement expressives

nized. In the *étude*, a mere 10 bars out of the 68 achieve even that limited melodiousness. Although both pieces are in a modified ternary form—ABA¹—*Mouvement* uses the melodic ideas as material for the establishment of the sections, whereas in the *étude* the example quoted above is itself a modification of the established material. The entrance of a tune, however limited its scope, controls the flow of energy from the demisemiquaver patterns rather as a lock controls the flow of a canal. It is easy to hear, in this *étude*, how the 'tune' drives the music to an ending, and to imagine that without it the patterns would have gone on for ever.

The ways of organizing the non-melodic material can be understood most clearly from looking at part of another *étude*, 'Pour les quartes'. The progression of ideas is perfectly satisfying to the ear and, while the variety is obvious, the unity is decidedly less so. As in *Reflets dans l'eau*, the answer lies in the treatment of direction and overall shape, rather than in details of interval (Ex. 43). In bar 1, the last two semiquavers of the group finally break upwards through a pentatonic pattern, but the grouping of the first two beats, in three pairs of semiquavers at successively lower pitches, is

79

Ex. 43

re-established by the cadence notes in bars 2–3, the successive lowering now greatly exaggerated. The dynamics of these notes are carefully graded so that the final chord blends; that is, the reinforcement of the upper harmonics by the final pair of notes is not drowned by the very volume of these notes. This vertical reinforcement is analogous to the horizontal reinforcement in his orchestral writing between unison sounds of different kinds, for example between cor anglais and cellos in the first movement of *La Mer* after Fig. 13.

The chord arrived at is composed of only four notes, with no semitonal clashes between them. Such aggregations, with a strong pentatonic sound, are static and, together with a rhythmic cessation, provide no possibility of growth. In bar 4, a second attempt is made. This time the 2nd and 3rd note pairs, in bar 5, are moved up a minor third, two semitonal clashes are set up and development is now possible. It begins with a clearer statement of the opposition between the first and third note-pairs, so far expressed only in static, chordal terms. The shape of the development has already been delineated in bar 1, starting on the 5th and 6th semiquavers and moving on to the first two of the next group. In bar 8, the last two beats are taken up by the opening shape of bar 1, prefaced by 4 notes which are melodically ornamental but rhymically structural, in that they keep the triplets in our memory. However, the bar ends on a root-position triad, as static a sound as the pentatonic one in bar 3. Once more, a second attempt is needed before development can prosper. Bar 9 is continued upwards, instead of arching back as in bars 7-8, and the rise is continued through to bar 11. In bar 10 the rhythm is an exact copy of that in bar 8, but in bar 11 the triplet takes over the second beat also. The highest point of pitch is reached in this bar and the line arches down again. However, the impetus of development from bar 7 pushes the music on for a further bar while a braking effect is achieved by concentration of material: bars 11 and 12 are organised ABC/BC/C.

Melodically, the music comes to a halt on the F sharp and the activation in bar 13 is both harmonic, textural and rhythmic. The chord held over from bar 12 is sharply dissonant, all the more so after the bland, almost faux-bourdon harmonies of the previous bars. The texture is enlivened by an entry in the bass register, unused for 3 bars, and the rhythm of this entry refers back, beyond the previous bar, to bar 11, where 2 beats including triplets were followed by one of duplets. In the mirroring of the overall shape of the rhythm—quick, quick, slow—rather than of its details, this technique obviously has close connections with the melodic one already observed.

Enough has been said to give at least an idea of the principles used in some of these later works. The generative technique can be viewed as just a denser type of cyclic variation in which every bar is relevant, even if vicariously, to the original idea, or as a compression of the ABAB¹ pattern of material mentioned on page 26. It also fits in with Debussy's declared admiration for the music of Mussorgsky, where 'the form consists of small, successive steps, linked in a mysterious way'. But, whatever its provenance, Debussy did not go on developing this style up to his death in 1918. In particular, he turned his back on many of the new sounds when he came to write the set of six sonatas for various instruments, of which only three were finished. In the last example, bars 7 and 8 illustrate a dichotomy of styles which perhaps suggests that all was not well. A comparison of bar 7 with the fourths in Ex. 36 shows a distinctly bolder technique after the interval of 5 years, while bar 8, on the other hand, could easily pass for one of the more lyrical and old-fashioned phrases in *Pelléas*.

This dichotomy is shown just as clearly from work to work;

between, for example, the *Trois Poèmes de Stéphane Mallarmé*, finished in 1913, and the Cello Sonata of two years later. Even if settings of Mallarmé are almost by definition 'difficult' and sonatas in the classical style more straightforward, the difference is still a disturbing one (Ex. 44). It is mirrored in his ambivalent attitude towards fellow-composers, especially

Ex. 44
(a)
Éventail *from* 'Trois Poèmes de Stéphane Mallarmé'

towards the young Stravinsky, who, like Debussy, was, in Debussy's own words, 'enlarging the boundaries of the permissible in the empire of sound' and so could be seen as a rival. The disparate elements in Debussy's music, so successfully fused in his middle years, became disparate once more.

If we look at Debussy's output expecting to see a clear line of development, we may find the late sonatas disappointing. What was, logically, the next stage after the *Études*? Perhaps for Debussy this question was a rhetorical one. He said of the Violin Sonata, 'One does not know whether to laugh or cry', a remark again indicative of contrary forces at work in his imagination. But against Debussy's own coolness towards the work we may set the fact that Webern thought it worth his while to analyse it, together with *L'Après-midi*. On the slender evidence available, it seems that Debussy might have turned away altogether from the world of sensations to that of abstract ideas, and if he had lived in good health for another twenty years there is no reason to be sure that he would not have produced music as revolutionary in that field as in the one he in fact made his own. We can be tolerably certain, at least, that it was not only patriotic sentiment but some deeper, artistic need which made him turn back in his last years to an avowedly classical style and sign himself 'Claude Debussy, musicien français'.

BIBLIOGRAPHICAL NOTE

General

Probably the best introduction in English to Debussy and his music is still Edward Lockspeiser's volume in the *Master Musicians* series (London, 1936). Jean Barraqué's *Debussy* (Paris, 1962) is also good, cheap, and contains some splendid illustrations, many of them not to be found elsewhere. The most complete general work is Lockspeiser's *Debussy, his life and mind* (London, 2 vols, 1962 and 1965), but to get the most out of it the reader should first acquire a fairly wide knowledge of the music. Also worth reading are Léon Vallas's *Claude Debussy et son temps* (Paris, 1932; 2nd edition 1958), and Marcel Dietschy's *La Passion de Claude Debussy* (Neuchâtel, 1962) which is a more serious work than the title might suggest.

The music

Articles of varying interest are to be found in:
Debussy et l'évolution de la musique au 20e siècle (Paris, 1965)
Special no. of *Revue de musicologie* (Paris, 1962)
Eleven articles on Debussy and his successors in *Musical Times* (London, Jan. 1967–Oct. 1968)

Piano music

Au piano avec Claude Debussy by Marguerite Long (Paris, 1960)
The Piano Works of Claude Debussy by E. Robert Schmitz (New York, 1950; reissued as Dover paperback, 1966)

Both writers were pupils of the composer and, whatever one's feelings about propagating 'tradition', they have many interesting things to say. Also worth reading is *Debussy's Piano Music* by Frank Dawes (London, 1969).

Debussy's own writings come under two headings:

Criticism

Monsieur Croche the Dilettante Hater is in *Three Classics in the Aesthetic of Music* (New York, 1962). It is a collection of articles he wrote for three magazines between 1901 and 1906. *Monsieur Croche et autres écrits* (Paris, 1971) is a complete edition of his critical writings. It also contains a number of interviews given by him to various newspapers.

Letters

Unhappily, there is no immediate prospect of a complete edition. Among the most illuminating are those in:
Lettres de Claude Debussy à son éditeur (Paris, 1927)
Lettres de Claude Debussy à deux amis (Paris, 1942)